Skiing with Confide...

Stunningly Simple Steps to

Overcome your

FEAR

on the Slopes and Transform your Skiing...

by

Kay Gill

About Me

As you'll read later on, I came to skiing relatively late in life at the age of 35. As a child I was always relatively sporty but skiing wasn't even in my parent's sphere of consciousness let alone their budget. When I eventually did get the opportunity to learn to ski at the local dry ski slope, I immediately loved it but was also immediately terrified.

Nowadays, I am a qualified, experienced Personal and Business Development Coach, Neuro Linguistic Programming Practitioner (NLP), creator of Red Shoes Coaching and rehabilitated fearful (actually scared s**tless) skier. I am also a fully trained Sports Massage Therapist with an excellent knowledge of human anatomy and physiology which means I understand how the body is designed to work **and** how the human mind works and the beautifully complex, intertwined way these relate to each other

My two greatest passions in life are people and skiing. Having learnt to ski against all odds I eventually overcame my crippling fear and totally fell in love with the sport, the mountain environment and the people I met there.

This passion plus my own personal experiences plus my expertise have driven me to produce this book and the accompanying website www.skiwithconfidence.com so that I can help all those other people who feel like I felt – nervous, anxious or downright terrified, to overcome their fear and bring joy and yeehaa's back to their skiing.

Why you should read this book

This book is for you if your fear and nervousness, anxiety or panic ruins your ski trips and stops you progressing. Maybe you get scared because -

You had an accident when skiing and are suffering a severe loss of confidence?

or

You were thrown in the deep end by some insensitive nerd when learning and have been frightened ever since

or

You've spent too long playing catch up with people skiing much too fast for you?

or...

You've actually no idea WHY you're scared – you just know you ARE!

I also know this is something you maybe don't tell people about, you may feel embarrassed and think no-one would understand. Well with this book and the free relaxation and visualisation recording that is also available for you, you can begin to conquer your fear in the safety of your own home.

I've purposefully made it easy to read and understand and really simple to implement. What you will learn will not only transform your skiing, it will also help you to gain more from any lessons you pay out for, it will help you progress and reach the goals and dreams you have for your skiing, whether that is to ski off piste, back country with your own personal guide or simply to get more fun and enjoyment from your holidays with family and friends.

Don't just take my word for it. You can imagine my joy when I receive unsolicited emails like this from people I've never even met ...

"I just wanted to drop you a line to thank you for your fantastic 'Skiing with Confidence' e-book. I read your tips before my holiday this year and they really did make all the difference. I can honestly say I experienced pure joy tackling red, and even a few black, slopes - all the while remembering to BREATHE!

For me it was the simplicity of your tips that made them so valuable - they were easy to remember and apply. There is so often a temptation to over-complicate things in life, so I applaud you for not going down that route!

I'm already counting down the months to next season! Will definitely be re-reading the tips before I head to the mountains, and I will wholeheartedly recommend the e-book to other tentative skiers I know.

I have also found myself unexpectedly applying your techniques in other areas of my life, which has been a great bonus. Thank you so much!"

Claire B

So... are you ready? Let's get started...

Disclaimer and Copyright

Dedicated to my children, Philip, Sophie and Russell, who unknowingly introduced me to skiing and opened up a world and a passion I would otherwise never have known.

Thank you xxx

Foreword

Kay's ski tips are really stunningly simple! After years of recreational skiing, when I read her book, I recognised all the little things that I did and thoughts I had that challenged me. Kay's style of writing is just like hearing her speak and I chuckled with amazement when, on my next ski holiday I found myself hearing Kay's voice say 'breathe'. Shouting and laughing as I skied made me breathe deeper and helped me get into the rhythm. No more self -talk on techniques – skis together, lean forward, up and down - as I skied, I just let out a yelp of enjoyment and it all came together. Taking it with me on the next trip!

Sandra Nundy,
Essentially Healthy,
Sheffield

Who am I to…

First of all let's get something clear… No – I'm not a qualified ski instructor – although I spent many years married to one and was once the proud holder of a 'Club Instructor' qualification that allowed me to teach beginners and early intermediates on the dry ski slopes in the UK (sheer bliss!) And No – I've never been near a writing course in any form – you will find that I write as I speak which may sometimes be grammatically incorrect but ALWAYS from the heart.

What I am however, is a rehabilitated terrified skier. I know from painful experience how some people, maybe you, feel when they're skiing. What's more – I've overcome that fear and I know how to do that! AND I'm passionate about helping other people to do the same and to pass on my knowledge and experience.

Of course, I do have certain skills that made all this possible. I am trained in Advanced Personal Development Coaching, Human Needs Psychology and Neuro Linguistic Programming. I'm also a qualified Sports Massage Therapist with an in depth knowledge of human anatomy and physiology so I trust you can see that I understand the human mind and body inside out and I know how the connection between the two rules our behaviour and our results.

Oh and just one more thing... I love books, especially 'how to' books, but I like them to be simple, easy to read and assimilate and to the point. And that's just what you'll get here. For the eternally curious or the scientifically driven amongst you I've made sure there are the answers to your 'WHY' and 'HOW does it work' questions but for those of you who just want to be told what to do, how to do it and when to do it, the simplicity of the list of tips at the back of this book is simply perfect.

How to use this book

Firstly, I suggest you sit down in comfort and safety and simply read it through from start to finish – maybe even a couple of times. I love a highlighter! Use one freely to capture your light bulb moments as they occur. Take time especially to highlight the tips that you instinctively know will work best for you. You will be naturally attracted to some – follow this intuition as these will be the ones to make the biggest initial improvement to your skiing experience.

Also – I have mostly skied in Europe where you ski on pistes, piste markers mark the piste and off piste is exactly what it says. But for my readers from outside Europe, please accept my apologies and my explanation that a piste is otherwise known as a trail.

To get the best from the book, use it in conjunction with the Skiing with Confidence Relaxation and Visualisation recording available to you from my website. There's a link from tip number 104 towards the end of this book that let's you get your own free copy downloaded straight to your hard drive.

Finally, when you head off on your next ski trip – TAKE THIS BOOK WITH YOU. Everyday choose two or three tips to focus on as you ski. Maybe take them from the same section so, for example, on the first day you simply focus on your breathing, the second your inner critic and so on.

'But I can't!'…

she wept – stuck, petrified on the top of a HUGE mogul… well in her mind it was anyway. She was stuck and had been for the past 15 minutes, unable to move, her muscles paralysed with FEAR. Tears were rolling down her cheeks, steaming up her goggles while her partner stood, swaying between offering help and advice to getting downright angry and thoroughly hacked off by her apparent stupidity. The kids meanwhile were embarrassed and unhappy with the argument that was brewing between the two, knowing that once again it was going to spill over into the evening making for another holiday nightmare. Eventually though, they were just getting bored by the whole situation, getting colder by the minute and simply wanted to ski!

In reality the slope I was on was well within my capabilities… the problem was that my fear way outstripped my ability, making every day of every holiday painful beyond belief.

My fear on the slopes affected, indeed infected my relationships with my friends and family.

Technically I was a good skier. I'd had so many lessons over the years I knew exactly what I should be doing. But everything went out of the window as soon as that irrational fear gripped me.

So – I'm curious...

How much time and money and energy have you wasted on lessons with instructors who addressed everything but the one thing that stopped you flying?

How many runs have you skied playing 'catch up' at the back of the class, getting more frustrated and panicky by the minute?

How many hours have you spent beating yourself up mentally for being so stupid, for holding everybody up, for spoiling their day/run/holiday/_____ fill in the blank!

How many times have you wished someone would just tell you **how** not to be afraid?

Well now you have the answers.

Contained within these pages are all the hints and tips no-one ever tells you, especially some of those flash instructors who are as sensitive to your feelings as a lump of wood, those guys who really don't want to spend their days with a whimpering wimp, the chaps who would really prefer to have a blast with the top, adventurous groups.

I'm certain you get my drift?

One of the things you're going to love most about this book is that the tips are written by me as someone who's been there, done that and got the tee shirt. Not simply someone who's learnt the theory.

Before I go any further I want to congratulate you for stepping up and admitting, maybe for the first time, that you get nervous – even scared, when you're skiing.

And that it gets in the way of your enjoyment of the sport you love!

But – if you learn one thing from this, simply know that you are not alone! I spent the first 12 years of my skiing journey being absolutely petrified! And it showed!

I learnt to ski against all odds at the not so tender age of 35. I never had any intention before then to learn to ski – in fact I was so unstable on any slippery surface that I'd fall over if they gave out a bad weather forecast! But luckily for me, as it turned out, a dry ski slope was built where I lived in Sheffield in the UK and before I knew it, some relatives had invited my three small children to try it out.

Spurred on by the fact that it seemed to hold great potential for future fun family holidays, I reluctantly agreed to take some lessons too. For the first few weeks, every night before my lesson the following day, I would lie in bed tense and terrified! My hands would be in tight fists and I would spend a fitful night skiing down the dry slope in my sleep.

Eventually though, amazingly, I came to love it! I was even good at it! But my fear stayed with me. Even though I knew the techniques, the why's and the how to's, my level of skiing and enjoyment remained stuck on a plateau due to my totally **IRRATIONAL FEAR.**

I know first hand just how debilitating irrational fear can be out there on the slopes. And what's more, I've since skied with many, many skiers who obviously felt just like I used to, even though many of them would never admit to it!

Of course, skiing can be scary! But there's a time and place for nervousness. It's useful, necessary even, to be aware of the dangers surrounding you out there in the mountains. They are real and to be treated with a certain amount of caution and a great deal of respect.

This **RATIONAL FEAR** serves to keep you safe.

But what I'm talking about here is the IRRATIONAL FEAR that inhibits you at every turn, even on those runs that are technically well within your skiing ability.

Irrational fear is exactly what it says on the tin! IRRATIONAL! I remember being asked by my daughter, who was only about 12 at the time, "Mum, what exactly are you afraid of?" I couldn't answer. There was no rational answer. Yes, I may fall, I may even hurt myself, but I knew this wasn't behind my fear. I KNEW I was a good skier. Yet I also knew I was being held back, controlled by this feeling that made every turn an effort, every run energy sapping and every holiday a nightmare for both myself, my family and my friends.

Over the years, skiing 3-4 weeks every season I failed to progress as I knew I should. And I spent a small fortune in the process. In the hunt for a miracle, I regularly bought new skis and new boots which I even sent off to America to have carefully fitted and aligned to my feet and legs. I went on course after course after course and had many a private lesson from instructors who seemed to want nothing more than to see how fast I could (or couldn't) go! Yet none of this helped, not one of those instructors noticed or addressed what was really holding me back… my fear.

So - What exactly is FEAR?

Simply put, *fear is an emotional response to your thoughts causing a physical reaction in your body.*

Rational fear serves to keep you safe. It's necessary to be aware when you are so far out of your comfort zone that you could be a danger to yourself or others.

In fact a little bit of fear is a good thing. It heightens awareness, focuses your attention and prepares you for action.

BUT, an overload of irrational fear will ruin both your skiing and your holiday.

In sports psychology this fear overload is explained in the Inverted U Theory of Performance (Yerkes and Dodson – 1908). The theory is this... as pressure is increased on the sports person then performance improves but only up to a certain point - this is the top of the inverted U. When the pressure increases beyond this point then performance is compromised by anxiety and stress.

When we apply this to skiing, at one end of the scale is total boredom, a run that really doesn't take any effort or focus to ski down, at the other end is sheer terror!! Those runs when your heart is pumping out of your chest, you start to sweat and your legs turn to jelly. And right there in the middle is the sweet spot, the area where you perform at your best.

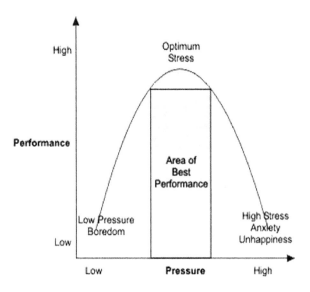

The Inverted-U relationship between pressure and performance

This sweet spot of performance is variable. It depends on both the skier's ability and their natural response levels to pressure. A beginner doesn't need much more additional pressure to overcook their performance, there's already enough pressure on them just getting used to the environment and the equipment.   FEAR exerts additional pressure just when it's least needed.

So how can you deal with irrational fear? The key lies in something I said earlier - my fear outstripped my capabilities. I was afraid even on a slope I could easily handle.

Let's take a look at how Fear affects you on a physical level.

These things you probably already notice

- Your heart beats faster
- Your breathing rate increases
- You feel the rush of adrenalin causing you to shake
- Your muscles stiffen and you become tense

These things you may not be aware of!

- Your field of vision narrows
- Your hearing is more focussed, peripheral noises are cut out.

- The little voice in your head (yes we all have one) –grows **LOUDER**!

Of course... there's a method to your body's madness. All of the above simply prepares you for 'fight or flight.'

Your heart and lungs give you more oxygen and your muscles are like coiled springs. Your vision narrowly focuses on the enemy, you only hear the noises you need to hear to keep you safe and your intuition is coming over loud and clear – when it says run – you RUN!

Now this is all very helpful when facing potential thugs up a dark alley but not at all helpful on the ski slopes.

- Just imagine the limitations...
- Tense muscles are hard to flex and are exhausting to ski with!
- Tunnel vision means you can't see other skiers or objects around you
- Restricted hearing makes it impossible to hear instruction
- And that loud little voice really isn't helping when it's calling you names!

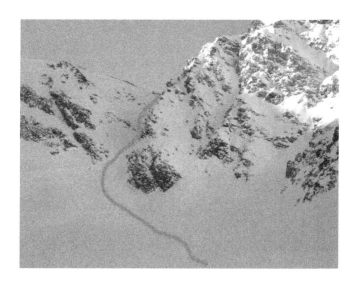

So how did I eventually conquer my fear and enable myself to ski slopes like this one?

YEEEHAA!!!   Now that's a great question!

What I learnt eventually came like a bolt from the blue...yet it had been there forever. You know how it is sometimes, when you're searching for something, you fail to realise it's been there in front of you all the time!

For all those years I had been expecting the answer, the miracle, to come from the outside, from some external source. Yet it wasn't in the books I read or the DVD's I watched or those poor instructors I expected to show me the Holy Grail.

No... the answer was there all along INSIDE ME! Inside my head, inside my body, hidden deep within my thoughts, buried in the deepest darkest recesses of my mind.

My Eureka moment came when I trained as a Personal and Business Development Coach and NLP Practitioner. I finally understood what was going on and how I could turn things around. I learned about 'State Management' from my great mentor Anthony Robbins, the wonderfulness of Hypnotic Language from the genius that is Milton Erickson. I read books like 'Feel the Fear and Do it Anyway' by the fabulous Susan Jeffers and 'The Inner Game of Skiing' by the insightful Timothy Gallwey and Bob Kreigel.

I came to understand that I could trust my body. I learned, or remembered, that my body knew how to stay upright on moving planks of wood if I would just let it. The answer was indeed so very simple – stunningly simple in fact, yet it took me 10 years and tens of thousands of pounds and dollars to learn.

Now heads up! Are you ready? Here's the secret to transforming your skiing!

The one simple fact you must know, learn and trust is this...

YOUR THOUGHTS CREATE YOUR REALITY!

Yes go on... re read that if you need to! And, if the small voice inside says 'well I knew that already' then good on ya! My question to you though is, if you know it already, why aren't you using that information to your advantage?

Whatever it is that is going on inside your mind is presented to the outside world through the way you use your body. If you don't believe me, think back to your last ride up a chair lift, you could easily spot those scared, nervous skiers below you couldn't you? You can spot them by their physiology

- the way they are using and holding their body.

So how does this translate into what YOU can and must do to transform your skiing?

Let me explain...

The basis of change comes from what I call...

The Three Cogs Of Transformation

These are your **PHYSIOLOGY**, your **FOCUS** and your **LANGUAGE** and together they create your **STATE**.

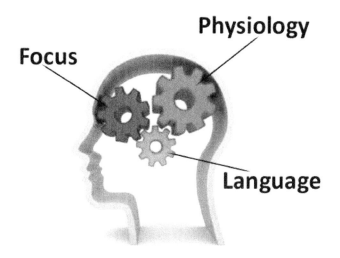

I call them **cogs** because you cannot change one without the others changing. They are interlinked and like cogs, if a change happens in one area, the other cogs are turned and every aspect changes. This is why massive changes happen simply by making one small adjustment to one area or cog.

Let's take a more in depth look at them. You can also learn more about them in the free Training Video Series on my site www.skiwithconfidence.com.

Physiology

Your physiology is how you use your body and what you need to know is that the way you use your physical body affects your body's chemistry. This includes every aspect of your physiology from your posture to your breathing, from the tension in your muscles to the expression on your face.

It is a well accepted scientific fact that exercise (aka moving your body), laughter (aka facial expressions and breathing) and even sex (aka... ok, let's not go there...) all produce those feel good neurotransmitters known as endorphins in our bodies. Each of these activities make you feel better, improve your state, because each one involves movement, relaxation and an increase in oxygen. A shift in your physiology will always, automatically create a shift in your state.

So here's a question for you. Can you tell simply by looking at someone whether they are feeling confident or not? Of course you can – but how? From their physiology of course, from the way they hold their body to the depth and speed of their breathing to other subtleties our brains perceive without us being consciously aware.

If you need further proof of this connection between your physiology and your feelings (state) do this simple exercise with me right now...

- Stand up and assume your being depressed position. That's right, your shoulders slump forward, head down, your breathing is slow and shallow.

- In this stance, what are you feeling? Yep – I bet your bottom dollar you are feeling pretty low.

- Now, stand up tall with your arms outstretched to the side. Look up towards the ceiling or the sky and put the biggest, most stupid grin on your face and continue to feel depressed.

If you played along with me there, what did you notice? That's right, it's impossible to feel depressed in the second stance. Your physiology dictates your feelings. Here's Charlie Brown's take on that courtesy of Charles M. Schulz...

Now then, have you ever noticed what happens to your body when you're having a bad day on the slopes? Maybe your head goes down, you drop your arms, your movements aren't efficient or effective because you seem to have somehow lost the power and energy you need to ski well.

What do you think would happen if you raised your head, stood strong and breathed deeply? That's right, your skiing will become more powerful, precise and pleasurable.

And NOTE: Changing your physiology the easiest place to start when wanting to change your state and the easiest way to change your physiology is by altering the way you are breathing.

If you learn nothing more from this book - learn this!

Be Aware of Your BREATHING!

This is the most important thing you will ever learn about how to ski without fear. DO NOT be fooled by its simplicity.

Breathing is known to be one of the most direct ways in which you can change your biological state in order to affect your neurology or, in other words, to change your state. Master your breathing and you will be a long way along the road to mastering your state and hence your emotions.

In the past I have been accused of this book being over simplistic. But in my view, if the information I present you with is easy to understand, learn and implement then the more effective it will be. Many teachers over complicate things in order to boost their own egos but that's not what I'm about. So yes, this may seem simple but celebrate that fact! This information that runs through the tips at the back of the book is the most important thing to remember when skiing.

B-R-E-A-T-H-E !

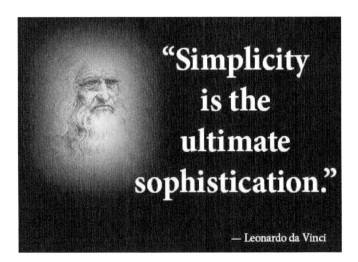

"Simplicity is the ultimate sophistication."

— Leonardo da Vinci

"Your method really works! It seems so simple that I didn't see how it could work. Yet, it did. We had wonderful, full days of skiing without any time lost due to me being frightened or upset. Thank you so much!"

Dr D Wirz, Neurologist
Connecticut , USA

Having said all that, I understand that some of you just need to know the 'WHY', so especially for you, here's the science...

Our breathing is partly under voluntary control and partly involuntary. This means that we can control our breathing consciously yet we also continue to breathe when we're asleep without having to think about it, that's what I call great design!

Also, our breathing rate is intertwined with the **sympathetic and parasympathetic nervous systems** within our **Autonomic nervous system (ANS)** which, as the name implies is automatic.

The function of the ANS is to prepare the body for and recover the body from stress and is made up of those two parts.

The Sympathetic Nervous System accelerates the heart rate, constricts blood vessels, and raises blood pressure. This is also known as the "fight or flight" response.

The Parasympathetic Nervous System slows the heart rate, increases intestinal and gland activity, and relaxes sphincter muscles and is often called the "relax and renew" response.

Now, the strongest sympathetic nervous system activator is said to be feelings of emotional distress. In other words FEAR! When you face extreme danger or severe threat (aka rational fear) or maybe just imagine you do (aka irrational fear), the sympathetic nervous system automatically makes changes in your body ready for your survival.

These changes include normalising your heart rate so that your blood circulates perfectly to supply oxygen and glucose to your body to help you to fight or run away from the threats, dilating your pupil for better vision and preventing you from loss of blood by increasing your blood clotting ability.

The Parasympathetic system is responsible for your body's ability to recuperate and return to a balanced state after experiencing that fear or stress.

Meanwhile your **Somatic nervous system**, over which you do have conscious control, allows us to make movements of our eyes, limbs, and mouths, for example, **as well as HOW (not whether) we breathe**. So it follows that you can, through conscious, somatic management of your breathing, affect which ANS branch remains active, especially during moments of stress.

But how?

One of the best means of inducing a relaxation response is through deep, diaphragmatic breathing (aka Belly Breathing). This is done by inhaling deeply through the chest and virtually into the stomach. The diaphragm is lowered and the belly moves out. It is thought that by engaging the diaphragm, a relaxation response is induced because the diaphragm is close to the Vagus nerve which supplies approximately 75% of all parasympathetic nerve fibres to the rest of the body, thus inducing the 'relax and renew' response.

On the other hand thoracic breathing, which is when you breathe high up in the chest, is associated with the sympathetic branch stress response.

If you're at all unsure of how to do deep, diaphragmatic breathing, watch a baby breathe. They do it naturally. To best teach yourself how to do this take a moment now to lie down on your back on the floor. Bend both knees and place the soles of your feet flat on the floor. Now, place the palm of your hand flat against your belly. Take a deep breath in and as you do push your belly out against your hand. As you exhale, force the breath out by letting your belly flatten again.

Many people have got so used to breathing using their upper chest that they find this incredibly difficult to do at first. These people may suffer with a feeling of almost constant stress, tiredness and fatigue and maybe a feeling of not being able to cope due to the low levels of oxygen being delivered to the brain through their poor breathing technique. They may also suffer from a range of breathing problems. If you're one of them make a point of practicing and honing this skill away from the ski slope. It will have a very positive effect on both your state, state of mind, your overall health and of course your skiing! Which neatly brings me on to...

Health & Fitness

Now of course, I can't talk about physiology without addressing the subject of your health and fitness can I?

Let's get one thing clear – skiing is a strenuous, physical activity. For many people preparation for their once a year trip to the slopes involves not much more than booking their holiday package and packing their gear.

After many months of almost no activity whatsoever, living and working a sedentary life they land, at altitude, in their chosen resort and immediately start throwing themselves into their skiing like there's no tomorrow. And unfortunately for one poor chap I heard of from my local town, there wasn't. The second day of his annual family ski trip, this being the day after a hard first day skiing followed by an equally hard night's drinking he collapsed and died of a heart attack out there on the slopes. You might be thinking, not a bad way to go, but this chap was only in his mid fifties – way too early to die.

I know you know what's coming next – yes – you must be fit to ski or at least to enjoy your skiing. If you're unfit both in your endurance and strength you will tire more easily. And when you're tired, your skiing will be compromised and your fear increases. So give yourself a chance! Start your fit to ski plan at least 6 weeks before your holiday. There are many programs and books out there specifically designed to help you get fit for skiing so you have NO excuse.

There is also one more invaluable fitness area to be addressed and that is your CORE STRENGTH. Having a strong centre, aka great core stability, is key to helping you ski well. Skiing is all about dynamic balance, the definition of which is your "ability to maintain a centre of gravity over a constantly changing base of support".

Simply put, this means that when you are skiing, you are often out of balance and you will use your core muscles to both stabilise yourself and return to your centre of gravity whenever possible.

There are many ways to strengthen your core. If you had no idea you even had core muscles or know they went their own way many years ago I would recommend you start by finding a GOOD Pilates class. My definition of good is one with small class numbers (8-9) and where the instructor has some form of Pilates qualification, if they are also a Physiotherapist that's even better. Check out the A.P.P.I (Australian Physiotherapy and Pilates Institute) for your nearest Instructor and if possible book a one to one appointment prior to joining a class.

My second recommendation is to get to know and love a Kettle bell. These fabulous pieces of kit are easy to use, can be used at home and therefore don't require you to go join a gym and they are superb for strengthening your core muscles. As with all exercise great technique is key and with these babies you must ensure you focus on having the right technique first before heading for the heavier weights.

Remember, improving your fitness will not only improve your skiing ability it will help you feel safe and in control and fear cannot live under those circumstances.

Hydration and its evil counterpart...

Have you noticed how thirsty you get when you're in a ski resort? The lower air pressure and low humidity found at altitude literally sucks water out of you. In fact at only 1800 meters (6000ft) you get rid of more than twice as much moisture as normal through your breath and sweat... and that's without adding the influence of extra exertion through skiing and extra layers of clothing.

What's more, the higher you go, the more you lose. Add to this the possible increased intake of alcohol you can see just how dehydrated your body can become and how quickly this can happen. Your muscles and your brain need water to keep functioning so give it a chance to do so by keeping yourself well hydrated.

Make a point of carrying water with you and taking sips at every opportunity. I use a system where I can carry water in a special bladder in my backpack which has a tube coming from it over my shoulder so that I can take a sip whenever I want without taking my pack off. I can easily drink a couple of litres during the day, especially in hot conditions or when skiing hard. I just want to give you a couple of heads up here – firstly if you get a system like this make sure the tube is insulated against the cold. There's nothing worse than finding your pipe is frozen at a crucial moment! Secondly, for those of you who are concerned about the possible increased need to go to the toilet remember that a) going to the toilet is a good thing but also b) You are replacing fluids already lost through your breathing and other bodily functions! This water is going to be sucked up by your depleted cells with relish. If you take small sips on a regular basis you won't find the need to be heading to the loo every couple of runs.

Drink your water before you start to feel thirsty, if you wait until you notice being thirsty you're more likely already dehydrated. Watch out for the signs of dehydration in yourself and the others within your group. These include:

- Headache
- Brain fog
- Dizziness

- Shortness of breath

- Nausea

- Fatigue

- Lack of perspiration

Focus

Your focus is basically where you are putting your attention.

We focus on what's OUT THERE and also on what's going on INTERNALLY and we get what we focus on! It's true! If you don't believe me take a look at this video here http://youtu.be/rzkp6upNyp8

I remember when I first watched that video – it absolutely amazed me. Now apply this principle to your skiing experiences. I've often wondered how skiers manage to hit trees or piste markers when they are often so few and far between! In fact, I even heard of a pretty horrific accident some years ago when a skier ran into a piste basher (snow groomer) back when they were allowed out onto the slopes during the day. I had to ask the question - How can someone NOT miss something that big?

Well, thinking back to what you learned in the video, when you are focussing hard on one thing in particular, everything else flies out of the window, add to this the negative self talk of 'I mustn't hit the tree/marker/pistie monster' and you can understand that your focus is pinpointed onto the very thing you want to miss!   You must learn to focus on what you want, on where you want to go.

I once had a very enjoyable day out learning to drive fast around a racetrack. Before we started the instructor told me what to do in case I got into a skid, 'Look in the direction of where you want the car to go' – simple! That is until I got out there on the track.

After a couple of steady laps, my confidence rose and my foot went down. Yeehaa! Great fun! That was until I was suddenly heading sideways at speed towards a concrete wall! My focus immediately went to what I didn't want to hit – and the car followed. It looked like there was no getting out of this unscathed. That is until the instructor reached over and forced my chin over to the other side, he literally forced me to look away from the wall and in the direction of the track. Slowly but surely the car turned, holding my nerve and the instructor my chin, the car followed my focus and disaster was averted – phew!

The lesson? Focus on where you WANT to go.

Here's another question for you

What do you see when you look at a mogul field?

Depending on your level of competence and your level of fear I predict you will either see a mass of MASSIVE bumps acting as an obstacle between where you are and where you want to go or...

You will see the path through the moguls leading you directly to where you want to go.

The choice is yours. You simply have to learn to change your PERCEPTION.

Per-cep-tion*: The ability to see, hear, or become aware of something through the senses or*
The state of being or process of becoming aware of something in such a way

Synonyms: realisation - understanding – comprehension

Even without having watched the video, you know that if you focus on something painful that has happened to you in the past you're going to feel pretty bad don't you? You may have even experienced this on the slopes, especially if you ski in the same resort often. You will have unconsciously made neuro-associations with some of the runs there. Maybe there's one run where you took a really bad fall, even injured yourself and if you think of it even now you may begin to feel panicky and tense. And of course this feeling will affect your emotions, your state and therefore your skiing.

So how does this all work? Well, our conscious mind cannot possibly take in and act upon the millions of gigabytes of input we receive every second so it has learned to filter out the unimportant information to create something more manageable.

The information is passed through three filters which are based on your beliefs, previous experiences, and your focus, what you are currently thinking about or looking for.

These filters are:

Distortion   Where more weight or importance is given to some aspects than others

Generalisation   Where one example is taken to be representative of a class of experience

Deletion   Where we leave some aspects out of the experience

As I mentioned earlier, the filters we individually apply are formed by our beliefs and experiences. If you believe you are a bad skier you will delete all the references you have to let you believe the opposite. You will distort the information by focussing on the times you skied badly and you have already generalised the situation by saying you are a bad skier. These three filters are going to be in action all the time, it's the only way our brains can work. So what can you do to make sure they support you instead of hindering your progress?

Remember what I said these filters were based on? Yes – your BEILIEFS and your EXPERIENCES. It's like we each see the world through our own pair of sunglasses, with each of us having different coloured lenses. The lenses we see the world through literally 'colour our world'. In NLP this is known as your 'Map of the World'.

So... Does this mean you're stuck with your perception of your skiing situation? Certainly not! You can absolutely change your filters and your beliefs. Even if you can't change your experiences, what has happened to you in the past, you can change the way you PERCIEVE it, you can change the meaning you attach to those experiences.

If you don't believe me, think back to when you were a child. Did you believe in Santa Claus? Do you still believe? I guess not. At some point you discovered those presents were put there by your parents and your beliefs changed in an instant.

And what's more important is you can change your beliefs simply by choosing new ones. Instead of believing you are a 'fearful skier who will never improve' how about choosing to believe right now that 'with the right attitude your skiing will transform instantly and you will continue to improve'?

Try it now...

Bring to mind a belief you hold, preferably one that hinders you or gets in the way of you enjoying your skiing. Now ask yourself 'What could I possibly prefer to believe about this?' and write down all the possible answers. Next, simply choose the new belief that is the easiest for you to adopt. You'll know this by checking in with the feelings you feel when you think it. Is it believable? Is it acceptable to your belligerent mind?

Now remind yourself of this new belief at every given opportunity. Speak it out loud, with emotion and you'll soon have it embedded within your unconscious mind.

Your **INTERNAL** focus works in the same way. These are your THOUGHTS and your IMAGINATION.

  Heads up! Here's another light bulb coming...

You Can Only Think One Thought at a Time

Or maybe two...

You Can Choose What You Think

Now there's a radical thought! Yes – YOU are in charge of what goes on in your head. You are in control.

And when you consider that feeling nervous, anxious or scared is usually linked to feeling a lack of control you will understand how those two light bulbs can and will, when put into practice, change your skiing forever. Think about it for a moment, when you are focussing on what you're doing wrong it is impossible to focus on what you're doing right. Simply shifting your internal focus will make a huge and immediate difference to your skiing.

I used to ski with a lovely lady who had been skiing for years, in fact she learnt to ski when the boots were made of leather and laced up and the skis really were very long planks of wood with crude bindings to attach them to the boots. However, she had spent the last 20 years following on after her fearless, fast and furious husband and three sons. This left her feeling inadequate, in the way, and absolutely petrified when she was skiing. Even though she was a very tidy skier, I could see the effect of this in her physiology out there on the hill.

I once asking her what she thought about when she was skiing, her response was immediate. "What if I hit that post?" What if I go over the edge of this run?" What if I catch an edge when I'm schussing and fall at speed?" The list went on and on. No wonder she was frightened. She was imagining every terrifying possibility that could potentially happen. It was like watching a horror movie on the screen of her mind.

'What if' is a very powerful question and, by the way, all of your thoughts are basically questions. Those two words can either limit you or open your mind to new and numerous opportunities. What did I do to help her?

I simply suggested she switched her question. For the next run I told her to ask the question 'What if I just ski this run the best I've ever skied it before and enjoy the ride?' I know by now you know what happened. She did exactly that, skiing beautifully, relaxed and in control.

Simple but not easy. Taming your brain, becoming conscious and aware of your thoughts is a skill. But any skill can be acquired and improved on with focus and practice.

Use Your Imagination - Visualise

Your imagination is an amazing tool. We think in pictures and we are free to imagine whatever we want to imagine. All new creations start as a thought, a picture in someone's mind. You have the power to imagine and create all manner of scenarios and as the saying goes 'What we think about, we bring about'. So it follows that if you are imagining falling over, having an accident, skiing badly then you really are setting yourself up for a poor experience.

It is a proven fact that your mind cannot tell the difference between imagining doing something and actually doing it and this recognised relationship between the psychological and the physiological has long been researched, proven and used in sports science and training. In fact, what is known as the Ideomotor response that described the similarities in electrochemical impulses that flow through a muscle when it is flexed and when it is 'imagined' to be flexed was first put forward way back in 1840's.

It is now accepted in the sporting world that we can prepare our bodies for movements long before we physically make those movements through visualisation or mental imagery or rehearsal as it is also known.

Therefore, you can ski a slope in your minds eye and effectively train your muscles to perform in a certain way. This is how and why the Relaxation and Visualisation recording in this program has such a powerful effect. Remember to download yours from the link at the end of this book.

Have you ever watched ski racers waiting to start? For most races, competitors aren't allowed to ski the course before hand, so they have to visualise it. They stand, eyes closed, skiing the course in their minds eye, visualising the turns, the bumps, where it gets steeper or where they need to let go and glide.

To continue with this theme...

Let's Pretend

Otherwise known, in the world of NLP, as 'Act as if' and this is plays a big part in the arena of modelling successful people. Once again, it brings your imagination into play and it can make huge, immediate changes in your skiing.

I remember following my young son, a fabulous skier at the age of 7 (I'm not bitter!) I imagined myself looking like I imagined he felt. I changed my posture (my physiology) to look and feel like him. I don't know if I looked as strange as I felt and to be honest I didn't care – because all I do know is I skied that run like no other before.

Language

Your language covers three areas, the language you use to yourself, the language you use with others and the language used by your inner critic, that small voice that resides in you head (yes, we all have one!)

These three areas of language will be radically different to each other. I'm pretty sure you use language to yourself, about yourself that you wouldn't dream of saying to a complete stranger. You know, those times when you berate yourself and call yourself names?

Your vocabulary is also key to shifting your state. Do this now, imagine something you really want to do or achieve, maybe, let's say, ski a red run with grace and poise and overflowing with confidence? Whilst imagining this say to yourself 'I hope I can do it'. As you speak, notice the energy in your body. How does 'hope' feel in your body?

Now, change that to 'I expect to do it'. Can you feel the difference? Which word is more powerful? Which word creates a more positive energy, a more empowered state?

How would you ski differently if you said to yourself before you set off 'I fully expect to ski this run to the best of my ability and have fun while I'm doing it!'? Even if there was no difference in your actual performance (which I'm actually pretty sure there would be) I'd bet my bottom dollar you would have enjoyed it more than if you'd have started at the top with the somewhat defeatist thought of 'I hope I can get down this'.

The language you use affects the way your feel, especially your internal dialogue.   Do you regularly berate yourself out there on the hill? How's that working out for you?

Your Inner Critic

Are you aware of the gremlin living inside your head?

That little voice, sometimes seemingly just out of earshot, often times talking so loudly you can't hear anything else? Also known as your Inner Critic, it really does think it's keeping you safe. Unfortunately, all you hear is criticism (or is it your Mother?!)

This small and sometimes not so quiet voice is the voice of your subconscious mind. Its language is based on your deeply held beliefs which as you now know, come from your past experiences and many of which you will be totally unaware of. If you listen to the language it uses it will be littered with 'shoulds' 'can'ts' and 'don'ts'. When you are experiencing fear it becomes louder. It simply needs to be heard because its job is to keep you safe, in other words to stop you doing new things that it has no experience of.

While your Gremlin certainly has a part to play, its presence unfortunately is more often inhibitive rather than liberating. Learning to be aware of your inner critic is a huge step to transformation and there are plenty of tips on how to deal with it on the slopes in the tips portion of this book.

Interestingly this is one of the most noticeable changes my one to one Skiing with Confidence coaching clients have when working with me. During the call I ask them to fully associate with being nervous and fearful and then check in with what's going on in their body and mind. I then get them to shake off that negativity and then fully associate with the feeling of being confident. Every client I have ever worked with notices a complete turn around with what their Gremlin is saying.

When Fearful, their Gremlins say things like "You have no right to be doing this, everyone would have a better time without you joining in. They'd do so much more skiing without you. You're a rubbish mother and girlfriend." or "Be careful … be cautious …. Don't do it" or "I can't do this"

However, when the clients are connected to their feeling of being calm and confident their Inner Critic changes its tune. Now it's saying "Let's go" or "You can do it" or more often then not it is totally quiet.

Also, beware of using words like ALWAYS or NEVER or CAN'T. Known as 'Universal Quantifiers', these are such decisive words – they leave no wiggle room for other possibilities. Remember, the language you use on a regular basis is constantly and consistently programming your subconscious which always wants to be proved right. To this end, your conscious mind will look for references to support those very definite things you always, never or can't do.

Changing the language and the vocabulary you use on a consistent basis alone will have a powerful, positive effect on your state and transform your skiing.

Back to the Cogs...

These three cogs together create your STATE. Your state is how you feel on a regular basis. How you feel really means the EMOTIONS you experience.

And, if you can change your state by a simple shift in your physiology, your focus and/or your language, surely that means that **YOU are in control of your emotions?**

Excellent!

But what is so important about managing your state?

When you understand that there is a connection between your emotions and your results then you realise that managing your state is key to your success.

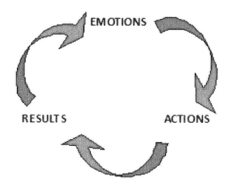

EMOTIONS

RESULTS   ACTIONS

Your **EMOTIONS** determine your **ACTIONS**
which create your **RESULTS** and the results
you achieve influence your **EMOTIONS**. This
can be a downward spiral if you don't take
control and change one of these elements.
Imagine you set out on your first run of the
day feeling nervous and lacking in
confidence. What do you think your skiing
will be like from that state? Yes, definitely
not great! I can almost guarantee you will
be tense, stiff legged, sitting back on your
skis and making cranky turns. Your results
will be pretty rubbish. You won't be flowing
down the hill, you may even make some

poor decisions piste-wise, you could well take a fall and even injure yourself. With that result, is your emotional state going to get better or worse? I know you know that without intervention you could spiral down, with each run getting increasingly worse.

Now let's look at the alternative scenario. You get up in the morning, get out on the hill and notice your nerves kick in. But now, instead of letting them determine some poor skiing action, what if you took a moment at the top of that first slope, which is, of course, going to be well within your capabilities and you decide to shift your physiology, your focus or your language to create a more empowering emotional state? That's right, you will ski with more fluidity, you will feel more in control and you will reach the bottom feeling a great sense of achievement.

And what do you think your next run will be like? You've got it, your previous result will influence your emotions, you'll be feeling successful, positive and more relaxed and when you ski from that state you'll be well on your way to having a fabulous day. Plus, when you're relaxed and enjoying yourself, you will be able to learn more easily and your skiing will improve quite naturally.

Find out how you DO fear

This is taken from the work I do with my one to one Ski with Confidence coaching clients and within my online coaching program at www.skiwithconfidence.com. Give it a go and discover how you use your Physiology; Focus and Language to 'do' Fear and Confidence.   Make sure you play full out and I think you'll be surprised by what you learn. Plus - I know you'll discover something that will transform your skiing next time you head to the mountains.

Imagine now that you are standing at the top of a slope that would **cause you to experience fear or nervousness**. Close your eyes if you wish, fully associate with the feelings and answer the following questions:

- What are you seeing? feeling? hearing?

- What do you hear? What is your inner voice saying?

- How does your body feel?

- How are you breathing?

** Shake the negative feelings off, say your telephone number backwards out loud **

(This serves to interrupt your state and gets rid of any negativity arising from the last question)

Now take yourself back now to a time when you were **absolutely confident** (either when skiing or performing some other task.) Stand as you stood then and answer the same questions:

- What are you seeing? feeling? hearing?

- What do you hear? What is your inner voice saying?

- How does your body feel?

- How are you breathing?

Now notice the differences. What is the biggest difference for you? What, if you were to implement it right now, would instantly take you to a state of confidence?

I trust that by now you've got a much better understanding of why you feel nervous or panicky when you're skiing and I know you're probably now wanting to know exactly HOW to make the changes you want to make? Well, great minds think alike, you've now arrived at my stunningly simple tips to change your state and overcome your fear.

As I suggested at the beginning of this book firstly, take the time to read through them all. Highlight the ones that switch on your light bulbs or those that you instinctively and intuitively know will help you the most. These really are the tips that will make the biggest, most immediate improvement to your skiing.

So, now you know the why's and wherefore's let's crack on with...

The Tips

1. If you learn nothing more from this book learn this - Remember to breathe!

2. Holding your breath makes you tense. Try it now. Stand up, take a deep breath in and hold... feel your shoulders, arms, neck, jaw, legs – how tense are they? Now imagine skiing like this. Ok – you can breathe out now. You cannot hold your breath and be relaxed at the same time.

3. BREATHE - Your muscles need oxygen to work, without it you'll get exhausted really quickly and suffer aching muscles the following day through lactic acid build up. Not a great plan!

4. Notice when you're holding your breath and whenever you do immediately breathe out. When you breathe out you naturally follow with a breath in.

5. Focus on your breathing – it keeps your mind off everything else!

6. Whistle while you're skiing. For a long time I couldn't even imagine doing this – then I realised why... I was holding my

breath. You simply can't hold your breath and whistle at the same time.

7. BREATHE!

8. Imagine your legs are like a pair of old fashioned bellows. As you stretch up you breathe in. As you flex your knees and ankles you breathe out. Imagine your breath smoothly flowing through your feet and out through your flattened toes.

9. Get into a rhythm of breathing. Breathe in, turn, breathe out; breathe in, turn, breathe out. Rinse and repeat. You'll be at the bottom of the run before you know it!

10. Breathe out when you get stuck.

11. Breathe out just before you set off. When racers push out through the start gates they all yell or scream or shout. Why? It's just their way of breathing out big style. Their next breath in will be massive and let's face it they need all the oxygen they can get to get them down the course.

12. Breathe to recover at the end of the run. Re-oxygenise and re-energise.

13. Oh and when would now be a good time to take a sip of water?

Be Aware of your Inner Voice

14. As always – awareness is key. Be aware of that small voice of doubt in your head – once aware of it you can change the dialogue.

15. Listen to what it's saying then say out loud 'Thank you for your concern but I'll take it from here.' It can help to give it/him/her a name. Mine is called 'Bert' because he often starts with 'Yes bu(r)t…'!

16. Change 'I can't' to 'I can'. Think you can or think you can't – either way you're right. Standing at the top of a slope saying 'I can't' isn't helpful! Your unconscious mind doesn't like to be proved wrong and will do everything in its power to be right. So set yourself up for success with the words 'I can ski this'.

17. Alter your belief from 'I don't know how to…' to 'I'm ready to learn'. Feel the different energy in those two sentences.

18. Give yourself a break! Stop berating yourself. When you hear the little voice in your head telling you you're

slow/rubbish/stupid or worse, tell it where to go!!

19. and BREATHE

20. Be kind to yourself. Treat yourself as you would a child or a stranger. Think about it, would you say the awful things you say to yourself to someone you'd just bumped into on the street? NO!

21. Congratulate yourself. Appreciate your successes. At the bottom of every run give yourself a pat on the back or a high five – seriously, I mean it – go on - actually do it!! (So you think you look stupid? Go to tip number 39)

22. Take a tip from Susan Jeffers' wonderful book 'Feel the Fear and Do It Anyway' and learn to tell yourself 'Whatever happens, I'll handle it'

It's All About Rhythm

Your skis are built for rhythmical skiing. They're made to store and utilise energy to move you easily from turn to turn. Be warned - rhythmical skiing is free flowing effortless fun – you're going to love it!

Skiing is all about energy and is physical in more than one way. When you are skiing you are utilising and playing with many of the Laws of Physics from gravity to momentum; from centripetal and centrifugal forces to kinetic and potential energy.

Learning to ski rhythmically will help you utilise these forces to your advantage and allow you to use the potential energy your skis were designed to harness. By linking your turns more effectively that energy will help you turn more efficiently, giving you more control and stability.

When you make long traverses between turns the potential energy in your ski dissipates making the next turn, when it eventually comes, clumsy and awkward. By practicing the following simple tips you will become not only less fearful but a far more efficient, effective skier.

23. Learn to count. Just try this – say out loud 'One and two and turn and one and two and turn' – all the way down the hill. This not only takes your mind off your fear but also creates the energy your skis need to turn more efficiently. And efficient skiing is happy skiing!

24. Sing and ski along to your favourite song. If you sing out loud it keeps you breathing too.

25. Choose a song of the day or a song of the week. You cannot ski, sing, smile and be fearful at the same time – try it if you don't believe me.

26. Spread a little happiness. Sing on the lifts (cable cars are the best!) When your song gets into the head of another fearful skier who then sings their way down the next slope you've made a difference.

27. Bounce! As you set off and between your turns bounce a little on your skis. This not only adds to your rhythm it also keeps your knees relaxed and able to flex and extend.

28. Remember to count! (see tip 23) This also means you don't have to decide when to turn – just do it to the rhythm. Have you ever traversed across the whole slope looking for the perfect place to turn only to find you eventually run out of piste and have to make an ugly, enforced turn at the edge? I certainly have! Not nice is it? The remedy? Simply count and turn and count and turn!

29. Change your rhythm. Think you can't do short turns – try this – One and turn and one and turn and one and turn – easy wasn't it?

30. Follow someone you trust and turn where they turn – feeeeel the rhythm.

31. Stay true to your rhythm then everyone behind you knows where you're going.

32. BREATHE out

Where's Your Focus?

As I mentioned earlier, there are two types of focus, internal focus and external focus. They are what it says on the tin.

So what are you focussing on externally? Here are my suggestions. The first is hopefully really obvious.

33. Focus on where you're going. Simple but effective. Well used by driving instructors to teach drivers how to get out of a skid. Simply look towards where you want to go and that's the way you will go.

34. Look for the path through the obstacles. Focussing on the obstacles themselves turns them into magnets. (You mean you didn't know trees are magnetic?)

35. and BREATHE

36. Focus on what you are doing – not what everybody else is doing nor what they could possibly be thinking about you. Believe me – they're not!

37. Notice how wide your peripheral vision is. Standing upright and looking straight ahead, stretch your arms out in front of you

with your hands together. Now, slowly move your arms out to each side of you. Notice when you can no longer see them. This is your peripheral vision. How far to the sides can you see? Fear narrows our vision. This used to help the cavemen when out hunting but definitely hinders on the slopes. The more you relax, the wider your vision, the more awareness you have of what's going on around you which in turn makes you more relaxed.

38. Remember – nobody is looking at you – you just think they are. Other people are just like you, whatever their level, they're focussing on what they're doing.

39. Follow someone you trust and turn when they turn – where's your focus now? I remember following a very nice ski instructor down the hill – you can imagine where my focus was – and it wasn't on how badly I was skiing!

40. Look ahead. If you can see your ski tips, lift up your chin and then lift it a little more. After all – you wouldn't drive your car looking at the bonnet would you? Imagine how scary that would be. I've noticed that 'little bit more' of chin lift makes a massive

difference to my skiing. I've not figured out the why – I don't need to! All I need to do is remember to do it.

41. Check out the skiers below from the chair lifts. Spot the nervous skiers – how do they look? How do you know they're scared? Next run down change whatever you need to so you don't look like they did.

42. Focus on the people in front of you, not what's going on behind. You wouldn't drive while constantly looking in your rear view mirror would you? So why ski focussing on what or who is behind you?

43. Firmly believe the person behind knows the rules – it's their job to miss you.

44. Give them a chance! Stick to your rhythm. Make it easy for them to know where you're going. If you suddenly stop – like a frightened rabbit – it's more likely they'll run into you. Come on – you must have done it in your car, been totally thrown by someone not doing what you fully expected them to? Stick to your rhythm!

Where Is Your Internal Focus?

It's a fact – you can only think of one thing at a time.

When you're focussing on what your body is doing you cannot be scared.

Here are some ideas to try out. Simply choose a different one on each run.

45. Focus internally on your feet. Where's the pressure? On the balls of your feet or the heels? Does it move between the two? If so when? If not, find a better instructor!

46. Unscrunch your toes. Remember the bellows? Breathe out through your toes. Flatten them as you bend your knees and ankles. Your boots will stay on without you gripping onto them. If not, find a better boot fitter!

47. BREATHE deeply

48. Drop your shoulders. Imagine there's a couple of strings attached to the bottom of your shoulder blades, pulling them gently back and down. Notice how this releases the tension.

49. Listen to your inner voice all the way down as though you are an outsider eavesdropping in on a conversation. Shout at it to go away as you make every turn (you can choose your own colourful vocabulary here!) So you feel stupid? Revisit point 36.

50. Sing out loud all the way down – no room in your head for fear now is there?

51. If at any time your feel out of control, simply stop, refocus and set off again. There is nothing wrong with stopping. The group you are skiing with will stop and regroup at some point and wait for you to join them. If not, find a kinder group!

52. Set your centre. By this I mean slightly tighten your deep stomach muscles. This really improves your balance. If you don't know how to or worse, don't feel you have any, consider going to Pilates classes before your trip.

Use Your Imagination - Visualise

Visualising your next run in a positive light before you set off will definitely set you up for success.

53. Take time out before and during your trip to relax and listen to the 'Skiing with Confidence Relaxation & Visualisation' recording which you can download here https://skiwithconfidence.com/relaxation-and-visualisation-recording/

54. Imagine how you're going to feel, how you want to feel. Relaxed, energised, confident, calm, in control, in the zone, flowing? Take your pick – what you see is what you get.

55. Visualise your route down the hill. If you've skied it before even better, you know the route – the bits you love and the parts you want to take it easy on.

56. Remember to BREATHE

57. Visualise yourself skiing beautifully through those 'sticky' patches. Everyone has certain areas of the hill they'd prefer to avoid. What happens in your minds eye when you know you can avoid it no longer?

Do you focus on the mess you made of it last time? Do you tense up? Not anymore you don't.

58. Imagine you are skiing like someone you admire. Pretend you are them. How do they look? How do they feel in their body? Where do they hold their arms? How do they hold their body? How are they breathing? What are their shoulders doing?

59. Act as if you are a great skier. Yep – just pretend. 'And now Mathew, for this run only, I will be…(fill in the blank)'

Take Up More Space

Now, for a long time I didn't get what this meant. What I now understand it to mean is to make your self bigger, both physically and attitudinally.

Physically, you can literally, make yourself bigger using your stance – that's the easy bit. Simply widen your stance to hip width and open up your upper body frame, widen your arms, round off your shoulders – think 'goalkeeper stance'.

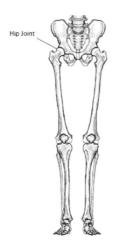

Hip Joint

Just one note on exactly what 'hip width' means. It is having your feet in line with the actual hip joint not the outer regions of your backside! This is where the ball of the femur (your thigh bone) fits into the pelvis, which is actually a lot narrower than most people imagine!

Attitudinally – claim your right to be on the slopes. Give out an air of certainty and authority – seriously – it works.

You can practice this at home walking through crowded streets. By simply altering your mind set to exude the feelings of 'I'm on my path, I'm coming through and I know exactly where I'm going', you will notice people move aside to let you through. You will be amazed! You may even get to like it!

Bonus Tip: If you don't yet feel certain and authoritative simply fake it till you make it. That's right, pretend you are. Your body will soon catch up with your mind.

60. Widen your arms and your stance. Frightened skiers ski with their elbows in, looking almost apologetic for being on the slopes. You have as much right as anyone else to be there – so assert your authority!

61. Widen your arms and your stance (part 2). Have your hands to the side and in front of you, just within your peripheral vision.

This gives you more stability and better balance making you feel more secure. (It's also technically better but I'll leave that for your instructor!)

62. Imagine you're in a large, impenetrable bubble as you ski, then make your bubble bigger and unpoppable.

Be Prepared

Your equipment including your skis, bindings, boots and poles are the connection between you and the snow. Your boots and bindings transfer your energy to the skis. The more precise the energy transfer the more precise your skiing will be and the more in control you will feel. Sloppy boots will dissipate the energy and you will feel you have to make bigger movements, usually feeling the need to use twisting movements in your legs or upper body to heave yourself round the turn. So take time out to get to know and understand your equipment.

Feeling safe and confident comes from being in control. Consider driving for a moment. If the road ahead is clear and dry you feel in control and your confidence is high. If you suddenly hit a patch of ice your control is immediately taken away and your fear comes screaming in.

Understanding your equipment and how it works will undoubtedly help you feel safe. I remember having a period of being fearful when flying. I understood that the main cause of my fear was a combination of having no control over flying the plane (not that it would've helped if I had!) but also having no clue of how this huge metal plane got off the ground let alone stayed up in the air!

Yet this fear instantly disappeared when I watched a TV program explaining exactly how planes fly! Just as getting to know how your equipment is built to assist your skiing will help alleviate your fears.

As this is potentially bigger than a few tips can cover I've put a fairly detailed overview at the end of the book. Go to Kit Yourself Out with the Right Equipment to read more on this topic.

More than likely you are one of the 1000's of skiers who hire your skis. These days it can make economical sense, especially if you have to fly to your resort and only get one week a year on snow. So how do you know what to ask for, where to get them and what to look for when you have? Even if you're buying skis many of these tips will still be relevant and certainly visit the section on equipment at the end of the book.

But for now let's start with your ski tips…

63. Understand that your skis have built in energy. They are made to turn. BUT… they are all built differently for different levels of ability, skiing styles and terrain. Your confidence expands with knowledge so take a trip to the back of the book for a little science and education.

64. Decide before you go what level of skier you are? Do yourself a huge favour and check out your level of ability in the **Get to know your equipment** chapter.

65. Choose your hire shop carefully. Don't be tempted to simply go along with whatever your tour operator suggests – they'll be making a handsome commission from any bookings they send the shops way so they won't always be acting in your best interests. If you're in a well known resort check the shops on line before you go or ask any skiing friends for recommendations. When you're there, check out their stock levels, what different levels of skis do they have for hire? Ask how old they are but watch out for flying pigs!

66. Be absolutely honest with yourself when evaluating your skiing. If you 'talk a good black run' but actually can't walk or should I say ski your talk, then expert skis will hinder rather than help you. Once again, check out the chapter at the end of these tips for more information on choosing your skis.

67. Understand that your skis have built in energy! They are made to turn! BUT... they are all built differently for different levels of ability. When hiring or buying your skis be really honest with yourself about your ability

68. When you've decided on the skis you want to hire check them over before leaving the shop. Here's what to look for

- Are the bases smooth? They should be free of gashes, holes and any deep(ish) scratches. You should be able to see a thin layer of fresh wax. If not – ask them to service them for you or get another pair.

- Are the edges sharp? Sharp edges help you turn, especially on hard, icy pistes. Best way to find out is to carefully run the flat surface of your nail across them. If the edge shaves off a very thin layer of nail they're sharp! If not – ask them to service them for you or get another pair!

69. Make sure they set your bindings up for YOU! I know it might not be your most favourite question to answer but when they ask your weight TELL THE TRUTH! If you tell them you weigh less than you do you will be popping out of your bindings right left and centre. Likewise if you say you're an expert, aggressive skier when you're not your bindings won't release properly when you fall.

70. Make sure your ski poles are the correct length. How? Stand in your boots, holding your pole upside down just below the basket. Touch the other end to the floor and check out your elbow. If it's at a right angle the length is fine. If not – get another pair. Too short a pole will be totally useless out there on the hill and too long a pole will be unwieldy and force you to sit back with every turn. I want to add an extra tip in here – and that is to learn to use your poles properly! Your poles offer an extra point of contact with the snow when turning which

means greater stability, a greater sense of control and increased confidence.

71. Take time to get a great pair of boots that fit well. If there's one piece of equipment I would recommend you buying it's your very own pair of good fitting boots. They will last for years and will become fine old friends. A good fitting pair doesn't necessarily mean they feel like a comfy pair of slippers! You want to feel secure at the heel. If possible when choosing, step into a pair of skis and lean forward, if your heel lifts significantly they're either too big or the wrong shape.

You can also take out the inner boot and pop this on by itself. This will tell you if you've got the right length.

Always wear the socks you're going to ski in when trying boots on and only ever wear ONE PAIR! Two pairs won't keep you warm but they will cause blisters.

72. If you're buying boots, get yourself along to a good quality shop with lots of choice and someone who knows what they're talking about! Go on a weekday when it's less crowded and phone up beforehand to

make an appointment. There are specialist shops that offer excellent boot fitting services and some who are specialists in skier alignment. Look out for them in your country – it's worth travelling and paying extra for.

73. When hiring any equipment remember – if you're not satisfied with it take it back until you are! If the shop assistants aren't helpful get noisy, kick up a fuss, get your money back and go elsewhere. It really is worth the time and effort to set yourself up for an enjoyable successful ski trip.

74 Make sure you have the best clothing you can afford or borrow. Being warm and dry keeps you relaxed.

75. Be prepared. To say the mountain weather can be unpredictable would be the understatement of the year. You can have all four seasons in one day. Take everything you might need with you. This includes:

- Goggles
- Sun Glasses
- Lens cleaning cloth
- Normal glasses (if you wear contacts)

- Sunscreen
- Muffler/scarf
- Gloves
- Hat
- Your LIFTPASS

Take Responsibility For Yourself

Know that you've got your own safety covered. Be responsible for yourself and your own safety.

No matter who you're skiing with, no matter who is leading the group, no matter if you are in ski school…

TAKE RESPONSIBILITY FOR YOURSELF.

76. Know where you are on the mountain at all times – there's no excuse.

77. Wear a helmet. They're quite 'de rigueur' nowadays and certainly help you feel very safe. Once you get used to wearing your helmet, to be without it is akin to driving without wearing your seat belt, you feel very unprotected and vulnerable.

78. Carry your own piste map

79. Learn to read a piste map! There is so much more information on a piste map than the names and grades of the runs. You will also find printed there:

- The telephone number for the ski patrol

- The closing time for all lifts

- Where to find emergency telephones, first aid posts and weather information. Also restaurants and other potential meeting places on the hill and ladies, even where the toilets are in some cases!

80. Understand the piste marker system in your ski area. The left hand piste markers are always different to the right. This means you will know, even in a white out whether you are on piste or unintentionally off piste. Look on your piste map for more information.

81. Take your phone with you and key in the number for the local piste security (to be found on the piste map). This isn't just for you're your own safety but also in case you come across an accident where those involved aren't quite as well prepared as you are.

82. Learn to recognise when you're tired.

83. Know when to say no and learn to say it. Practise now - 'I've had enough now and I'm going to stop' or 'No thanks, that run is way beyond my ability at the moment, I'll take the other route down' or even simply 'No thanks – I don't want to'. As they say – pride comes before a fall!

84. Know when to stop, both on a run or at the end of the session. More accidents occur after the words 'Go on then – just one more run' than any others!

Choose Who You Ski With

It's unfortunate but true - skiing can sometimes bring out the worst in people.

I've skied with some wonderful people who become like Jekyll and Hyde as soon as they step into their bindings.

Off the slopes they are courteous, considerate, kind and fun to be around. On the slopes they become monsters with no consideration for anyone else.

What causes this? FEAR – Yes they're as scared as you are! Maybe you'll be kind enough to lend them this book?

85. Choose a group to suit your ability

86. Spend 70% of your time in your comfort zone and 30% just outside, in your s-t-r-e-t-c-h zone.

87. BREATHE

88. Park your pride and move down a level if needs be. Hurt pride is a lot cheaper than a rubbish holiday or a long hospital stay!

89. Remember – every body is a learner and the ones that don't know this usually have more to learn than most.

90. Ski with different people so you're not always at the back

91. Get behind the instructor as often as possible if you're in lessons. For an added bonus revisit tip 39

92. and BREATHE

93. Do everything you can to ENJOY your holiday!!! It's YOURS – you paid for it.

Set Yourself up for Success

Your success is inevitable if you follow the tips I've offered you throughout this book. BUT your success is also DEPENDANT on you following through on them. To help you further to set yourself up for success both before you go and during your ski trip I've added these bonus tips...

94. Set Yourself up for Success with a Great Supporter! Who knows about your fear and nervousness, your lack of confidence? Have you shared your feelings with anyone? Who have you specifically told? Choose someone who you would you like to support you while you're away. Brainstorm some names. Who is the perfect person to support you? Choose the best person for YOU.

95. Consider how you would like them to support you? What do you need? Hugs? Laughter? Trust? Tough love?

96. Decide how you will ask for their support. When will you ask them? What will you say? Make sure you get across everything you need them to know – write it down if necessary so they fully understand

what you need from them. Get their commitment to help you.

97. Now book a time and place to have that conversation. Tell your supporter exactly what you need! Make sure they hear, understand and know what you want and need them to do to support you.

98. Set Yourself up for Success while you're away

- Take your book and recording with you – and USE them

- Take a journal with you and use it to capture your successes and improvements

- Everyday choose 2-3 tips to use throughout the day and USE them

99. Review Your Day – at the end of EVERY day answer the following questions, preferably write your answers down in your journal so you can track your progress:

1. What went well?

2. What were you pleased about?

3. How did you feel?

4. What successes did you enjoy?

5. What would you like to improve on?

6. What will you do differently tomorrow?

7. Are you having FUN?

8. How close are you to achieving your goal? Use a scale of 1 – 10, (where 10 is 'fully achieved it' and 1 is 'nowhere near'!)

And Relax…

OK – I know that's easier said than done but by now you should be getting the hang of it!

100. Remember the first rule of fearless skiing - BREATHE

101. Take a break when you need one. Skiing with tired legs isn't pleasurable, clever or pretty.

102. Laugh. Don't take yourself so seriously.

103. Have FUN (are you getting the common theme here?)

104. Learn how to relax easily off the slopes by listening to the 'Skiing with Confidence Relaxation & Visualisation' recording available here http://skiwithconfidence.com/relaxation-and-visualisation-recording.

105. Chill out on the chair lifts – start singing your song of the week and see who joins in

106. Take in the views – WOW! Nature at her best.

107. Play games – synchronised skiing anyone?

108. Remember, you're doing this for the sheer joy of it. If you're not then you're in the wrong place!

109. and finally... yep – you've got it...BREATHE!

Kit Yourself Out with the Right Equipment

As I said earlier, understanding HOW a plane can fly helped me lose my nerves when flying. Knowing how your skis are made to work may help you be a more confident skier. And as I said earlier, your skis have built in energy. They were built to turn! BUT... they are all built differently for varying levels of ability.

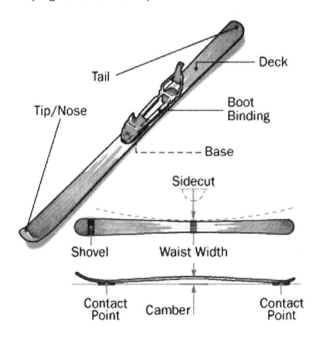

In very simplistic terms your ski, whether it has a camber or a rocker construction, is made so that when it is put on its edge and has a constant pressure applied will track around a pre-determined arc.

However, the sidecut of your ski will determine the radius of the arc and where the most energy is stored in the ski.

To discover how individual skis will behave, check out the numbers printed on the upper side. You will find:

- Length (cms)

- Radius (metres)

- Tip width (mm)

- Underfoot or waist width (mm)

- Tail width (mm)

 The last three will appear as a set looking something like this…

123 : 72 : 105

OK – are you ready for some science?

The ski length is mainly determined to a degree by your height and is fairly easy to understand – the shorter the ski (relative to your height) the more manoeuvrable and agile they'll be, giving quicker response from turn to turn.

The radius determines the size of the curve the skis are built to make naturally when set on their edges. The smaller the radius, the tighter the turn which gives easier speed control and greater manoeuvrability.

And those three little numbers?

These determine where the most energy is held in the ski. Your skis have potential energy. They only really mean anything in relation to each other. Together they tell you what the sidecut of your ski is and the sidecut determines how your ski will work when set on its edge. Now stay with me here – this is really useful stuff that not many people know and even less understand!

A comparatively wide flare at the ski tip means that the ski will engage in turns very quickly and the arc of the turn will be tight.

A comparatively wide flare at the tail of the ski means the ski will hold steady at the end of the turn because of its 'rudder effect'

You can therefore figure out which part of the ski will be doing most of the work for you.

Using the numbers from my own skis to give you an example, we can find out where the energy 'sweet spot' is on my skis – and what this means.

Here are the figures

- Tips = 123 mm

- Tails = 105mm

- Waist 72mm

The Tip flare equals the Tip minus the Waist which is -

123 - 72 = 51mm

The Tail flare equals the Tail minus the Waist which is -

105 – 72 = 33 mm

and...

Tip flare divided by Tail flare = the Energy Sweet Spot

OK – still with me?

Therefore on my skis 51/33 gives me a ratio of **1.54 : 1**

Meaning my ski will distribute **54%** of its turning energy towards the front rather than the back, making my skis easier to initiate a turn and they don't catch me off guard when I relax a bit and maybe sit back a little. In essence this ski is quite forgiving and doesn't mean I have to be skiing aggressively all the time.

Bearing in mind your level of skiing where do you want most of the turning energy?

Beginners tend to sit back – there's no getting away from that. so they will want all the turning help they can get. A 'front loaded ski' will help them turn more easily and be very forgiving. It also means the tails will have a little relaxation, a skiddy-ability and won't power them out of a turn giving rise to a feeling of being out of control.

If you're a fit, aggressive, expert level skier willing to work the skis all day long go for a more evenly balanced ski but be warned – you'll get a big thrill but no relaxation!

Just remember...

Tip energy is designed to start the turn

Tail energy is designed to hold the curve

Phew! And BREATHE. Well done – now onto easier stuff...

Whether you are looking to hire or buy your skis there are a few things to consider beforehand. The first thing is to remember that men's and women's skis are designed differently. This is not a case of the manufacturers being sexist or that the women's skis come in prettier colours!

No - in case you haven't noticed, men and women have physiological differences which make us ski differently and the gender specific skis are built to function more efficiently for the two sexes. Vive la difference!!!

Next, to determine the best skis for you, you must answer these two simple questions:

- **At what skill level do you typically ski?**

- **Where and in what conditions to you most often ski?**

The key here is to answer these questions with honesty! They're not asking what level would you love to be? Or are you really an off-piste beast in sheep's clothing?

Getting the right ski for your current ability will help you to progress quicker than if you were to use a more advanced ski and discover that it's akin to riding a bucking bronco! Yes – you may aspire to ski off piste, in fact it's great to try the soft stuff out at the side of the piste at every opportunity if that's your goal. But do not be tempted to get the fat powder skis if you're still mastering carving up the groomed pistes. One mantra I love to keep in mind is...

'You are where you are and that's ok'

Acceptance is a wonderful thing. Accepting your skill level and indeed your confidence level, creates the perfect base to support your development.

Know your Skiing Level

As I already mentioned, picking a ski that's either above or below your level can seriously impede your ability to improve both physically and mentally. Advanced level skis are stiffer and require more technique, but they respond quicker. Conversely, beginner to intermediate skis are softer and more forgiving, making them easier to initiate a turn at slower speeds with less technique; at high speeds, however, they can create a lot of chatter, making them hard to control. There are six different levels of skiing ability that you may be classified under. From lowest to highest, the levels are Beginner, Advanced Beginner, Intermediate, Advanced Intermediate, Advanced, and Expert. The key is to pick a range that you are comfortable with, but one that you can also improve with.

Beginner: This is an easy one! You have either never skied before or has skied only a few times. You make snow plough turns on easy, groomed terrain. You will be cautious and still learning basic control.

Advanced Beginner: You are happy on the beginner runs and are moving on to the intermediate runs. You are managing to sometimes finish your turns off with your skis parallel but you will initiate the turn using a wedge.

Intermediate: You now ski groomed intermediate runs with relative ease and your focus is on making parallel turns even though sometimes you use a small wedge before you turn. You are still cautious on more challenging runs and are comfortable at moderate speeds. Athletic beginners will also benefit from skis designed for intermediate skiers

Advanced Intermediate: You have now conquered the intermediate runs, are comfortable skiing on most terrain at moderate to higher speeds. You may be happy and eager to venture onto the more advanced slopes in good conditions.

Advanced: You are comfortable skiing expert runs and varied terrain. You are able to make large and small radius carved turns at higher speeds on advanced terrain. You are able to ski in control at higher speeds, but don't always ski aggressively.

Expert: You can ski anything anywhere. You have strong technique, prefer to ski aggressively and probably really don't need to be reading this book!

The key is to choose a ski in the range that you are comfortable with, but one you can also improve with.   Look for a pair with your level at the lower end of the range.

I re-iterate, there is no advantage to having a ski that is significantly better than you. More advanced skis must be worked hard to get them to work effectively. If you can't achieve the right speed and pressure the skis will be difficult to control and will not enhance your skill or confidence.

Ski Conditions

If you ski mainly on groomed terrain you'll want a ski with a fairly narrow waist to help you get great edge control and carve out your turns. A narrow waist is usually between 75 – 90 mm under the foot.

If you like to spend time in the powder and crud then you would be better suited with a wider waist but again – you're probably not reading this book!

The key here is to make sure the person selling or renting your skis to you understands how and where you like to ski.

Ski Length

This has become increasingly confusing with the advent of shaped skis. The typical length of skis has changed, gone are the days of skis towering over your head. This is because the hourglass shape of the ski allows for a shorter ski with a wider and larger surface area. These skis were born to turn more easily and are much more stable due to their shape and new materials.

As a general rule, a ski should reach up to the chin for beginners, the nose for intermediates, and the forehead for advanced skiers.

There are of course some exceptions. Heavier skiers will need a longer ski, while lighter skiers can go a bit shorter.

Of course, if you're hiring your skis you can always head back to the shop and change them if you're not happy. And if you're buying look for the shops that allow you to try before you buy.

So there you have it...

My stunningly simple tips to overcome your fear on the slopes and transform your skiing without wasting more time and more money on more lessons with no progress.

To finish, I want to share with you the very best definition of skiing I ever heard.

This is it:

SKIING IS SIMPLY A SERIES OF LINKED RECOVERIES

This helped me enormously. I came to realise that when you are skiing you are off balance for much of the time, very much like life really, and that's OK!

In fact, as you read through these tips again, you will notice many of them are equally as relevant to your life off the slopes as the time you spend on them.

Imagine how different your life would be if you simply chose to adopt a few of these tips.

For instance, when was the last time you congratulated yourself for a job well done? Or changed your language to include 'I CAN DO IT' or to focus on your future instead of your past and finally – yep you've got it, to simply breathe out when you're stressed.

I know you came to this book with the serious intent of getting more fun out of your skiing.

I know you'll leave it with the bonus of some serious knowledge of how to get more fun out of your life.

And finally... can I ask a favour?

I see you've made it all the way through to the end of my book. I'm so glad you enjoyed it enough to read it all and wondered if you would be open to leaving me a 4 or 5 star review on Amazon? You see, having people like you give me reviews really helps me a lot to reach more people and help them to Ski with Confidence.

Thank you so much. It really means a lot to me. Please remember to download your free Relaxation and Visualisation Recording here http://skiwithconfidence.com/relaxation-and-visualisation-recording with my compliments. Wishing you happy, confident skiing!

Printed in Great Britain
by Amazon

18549755R00068